The Scent of Spring,
Elegies out of Season

THE SCENT OF SPRING,
ELEGIES OUT OF SEASON
KAREN MULHALLEN

THE **BLACK SPRING**
PRESS GROUP

First published in 2022
An Eyewear Publishing book, The Black Spring Press Group
Grantully Road, Maida Vale, London W9
United Kingdom

Typesetting User Design, Illustration and Typesetting, UK
Cover art 'Harpoon Bear' (2012) with permission of the sculptor John McEwen

The author of these poems has requested we use Canadian spelling and grammar

ISBN-13 978-1-913606-59-6

For all those in the struggle for justice
To all those who have gone before

CONTENTS

I
MOSUL,
CHILD AND BICYCLE

In the foreground, a child rides his bicycle
moving left to right, across the frame.
He is pedaling, standing up over its black seat,
hands gripping handlebars. Over a red T-shirt
he wears a black and grey hoodie.

Yet the stone and metal rubble,
piled on the ground to the right of the silver bicycle,
in the forefront of the photograph,
suggests this is not just a little boy, on his bicycle
taking a leisurely afternoon ride.

The boy looks toward the camera,
toward the unseen photographer.
Above his head, suspended like an angel,
like a hovering cherub,
pointed in the same direction as his bicycle,
is a black car with silver spoked tire caps.

The car is driverless.
Where have the passengers and driver gone?
Are they in the mosque praying, or taking shelter,
looking out from the famous leaning minaret?

Behind the airborne car, in the middle ground of the photograph,
is an orange car, pointed in the opposite direction,
its trunk sunk beneath rubble, its roof torn open

above the driver's seat, its glass windows vanished,
resting on its tire barrels, aslant the heaped stone remains
of somebody's home in the old city of Mosul.

Leaning in an open doorway—a collapsed window frame,
nearer the boy on the ground—a green and white patchwork quilt.
Where is the family who fled the scene,
leaving behind in the ruins a family treasure,
the grandmother's quilt?
Where is the family the boy pedals toward,
or is he simply fleeing the helicopters, shelling,
car bombs and troops, those Iraqi forces
liberating the Old City?

Is he, like hundreds of thousands, and thousands,
fleeing the muddy streets in search of water, food, shelter?
Is he running away from snipers, suicide bombers?
Is he pedaling away from the stench of the decaying bodies
left to rot in the blazing sun?
The famous leaning minaret is gone, reduced to a stump,
with the Grand Al-Nuri Mosque.

Looking at the camera, does the boy wonder
if the camera is a gun, this his own final moment?
In the background, the world is collapsed grey stone:
here, a window, there, a roof,
here, an elegant fan light, and what was once
a hopeful pale green plastered façade.

I sat in my home, on a Monday morning, drinking coffee.
Early morning, nearly spring,
and the light, already improbably strong,

spreading evenly across my newspaper,
and the boy on his silver bicycle
lying on my Italian marble, rose aurora, dining table.
Not the light in the photograph of the boy in Mosul
pedaling through the wreckage of his home town.

The view out of my western window—
my neighbours' green swards,
tidy façades, proudly tended front gardens,
and two or three little dogs, taking morning walks,
their owners safely tethered
to the ends of their leashes.

II

GRASSY NARROWS
An Idyll in Eight Parts
on
the English–Wabigoon River System

Everything was disappearing

Prologue

A sunny day on my computer screen,
as people fish from a river

moving in concert, with tranquility,
as they always have.

They place fresh fish on twigs
holding them to cook over open fires.

From time beyond memory, the river has sustained these people.
They gather as a family, as a community,

thanking the river for food.
Food we fishing tourists now refuse.

In the beginning, a homeland.
For millennia people lived here, lived from this place.

They eat from the land, drink from the water,
fish from the river.

Hunting, fishing, picking blueberries, gathering wild rice,
making plant medicines, harmony.

People, land, water—interconnected, honoured,
a land of plenty, all in touch with its spirits.

Then came the *nakba*.

In the 1960s, and early '70s, 9000 kilos of methyl mercury,
toxic heavy metal, dumped by Reed Paper into the English–Wabigoon Rivers.

Upstream, on the mill site, in Dryden, Ontario,
was a secret mercury dump.

Five decades pass, the *nakba* continues,
unending mercury,

leaching into soil, river, fish, water, humans
on the English–Wabigoon Rivers.

I

Former Chief of Grassy Narrows,
Simon Fobister has trouble walking,
talking, eating, swallowing.

2014, he comes to the Legislature, pitches his tent,
speaks to the press—
Can't even button my shirts, or put on my shoes.

In pain, Fobister's body is breaking down from mercury poisoning.
Japanese experts, Dr Masazumi Harada and others concur—
Minamata disease.

Yet Simon Fobister knows what you think when you see him—
another drunken Indian.

Before I die, I hope we can eat from our land.
This is home. I am afraid for our culture,
our homeland, our health.

The poison is invisible, but visible—
We are the poisoned people of Grassy Narrows,
living on bottled water, full of plastic microparticles.

Our community grows—
welfare cheques pegged to numbers,
800 of us now—while the river is dying.

Our elders, our wise ones, have passed over.
Our community is sick.
Our culture disappearing.

Our children, my five grandchildren,
suffer seizures, understand nothing.

II

July 2017, Simon Fobister begins a hunger strike
against government inaction:

Our walleye are sacred, more than human.
Our pickerel teach us wisdom.
How can something that good turn against us?

The river was our highway.
We were self-sufficient, jobs, food;
now we are dependent on the monetary system.

Why have you dumped poison into our living body?
We keep eating fish.
Fish are what we have to eat.

When our fish are safe to eat, we will know
Ottawa has kept its word:
the mercury is gone.

III

October 2018, another former Chief Steve Fobister is now dead.
Wrapped in two blankets, first a white one, then a black one,
each adorned with indigenous designs,
he is buried.

Family members are told—
Walk to your vehicles.
Do not look back.

IV

2019, people with walkers and canes
navigate the dirt roads of Grassy Narrows
hoping to meet with government officials.

Judy da Silva, community health worker, walks with a cane.
She has lost sensation in part of her face.

There is no hospital in Grassy Narrows.
The drive to Winnipeg takes over three hours.

V

Chief Rudy Turtle has lost faith in government,
in parties promising at each election to help.

While journalists for decades cruise up
and down the Jones Road, due north of Kenora,

we fit into the land,
to be indigenous is to respect,
to belong to the land.

In 1871, we made a treaty to live in peace.
The land, hunting, fishing, all given to us:

Now elders die, children sicken.
Nothing to look forward to.
Sickness in our land.

VI
Interlude
June 2019

A summer day, noon, a threat of rain.
I am standing on the grass in front of the Ontario Legislature,
Queen's Park, Toronto. The River Run Protest.

The people of Grassy Narrows have travelled 1700 kilometres
to build awareness of the injustice done to Grassy Narrows,
to pollution, to government inaction.

On the west side of Queen's Park are wheelchairs,
many people in blue T-shirts symbolizing the river,
from which the people of Grassy Narrows live.
About twenty police, most in shorts, some on bicycles,
mass near the legislature.

The people of Grassy Narrows make a big circle, the circle of life,
as they drum gently, singing their national anthem.
Some of the women of Grassy Narrows wear ribbon skirts.

At the microphone, the speakers are soft,
I strain to hear them, although I am only a short distance away.
We give thanks to our ancestors
and we give to you unconditional love.

You can go without food for a long time, but water is necessary.
We ask Prime Minister Trudeau to compensate us for the mercury.
We ask for a health centre, and the clean-up of our land and waters.

We will not move, we have lived here for thousands of years:
We are people of the river, we live from the river:
Grassy Narrows, River Run.

VII

The young people of Grassy Narrows,
the N'we Jinan artists are singing on YouTube,
spreading the word:
Ogagwejimaan, ogagwejimaan

Don't believe everything you hear
It's a long road, but we'll get there
Grassy Narrows: Home to Me

We held onto our culture
It's calling us back

We'll rise from the ruins
We are connected to the land

We are one with each other
Don't believe everything you hear

It's a long road, but we'll get there
Rise from the ruins
Connected to the land
We're one with each other

It's a long road, but we'll get there
We've held onto our culture
It's calling us back

Honour our rights
         to Grassy Narrows
Honour our forests.
            no clear-cut logging
Honour our rights
            to clean water
Restore our lands

A place to regain who we are
Asubpeeschoseewagong
Asubpeeschoseewagong

III

THE PIGS IN QUESTION

I have been thinking about pigs, about bearing witness for pigs
and about hiding the little pigs, as they walked to slaughter.

And about this little piggy who went to market,
And this little piggy who stayed home,
And this little piggy who, they say, ate roast beef,
And this little piggy who had none,
And this little piggy who went wee wee wee wee

All the way home,

And the 180 little pigs in the overturned truck,
And the 40 who died in the crash
And the 140 little pigs who were walked to the slaughter house
Going wee wee wee wee;

Or was it the laughter house
hidden behind large cardboard placards,
held by slaughter house employees
who herded the escaped little pigs to market,
to the gas chambers,
where they won't be able to breathe,
their little trotters flailing against the cages,
as they are slowly lowered into the gas, humanely,
that is according to human values,
where they slowly, painfully, asphyxiate,
as they scream wee wee wee wee:

And one woman alone tried to save them,
while they walked free on the sidewalks of Burlington,
and I didn't expect, as it was Thanksgiving week,
that that woman, Anita Krajnc, would be arrested,
hand-cuffed, taken by force by the police
for trying to walk with the little pigs to freedom.
Compassion is not a crime.

And I found it odd that the very next day,
when I went to Barbara Edwards Contemporary,
an art gallery just up the street from my home in Toronto,
there were pigs everywhere
as if they had escaped the gas chambers
in the slaughter house in Burlington
and found their freedom in art
and maybe in a poem.

And all those facts about pigs which we know—
how they're smart, really smart,
and affectionate
and how we demonize them,
calling bad bad people pigs;

And we suggest pigs are dirty and stinky and sweaty,
when we know it's all about us, we are
dirty and stinky and sweaty.

We are the wolves that
blow their houses down and
eat the industrious little pigs.

In England, in the 18th century, there was a famous pig.
He was called The Learned Pig, The Sapient Pig,
known for his counting skills;
he spelled words, picked up cards in his mouth,
answered arithmetical problems.
He was also called The Wonderful Pig.
He read time and people's thoughts.
His owner prized him, and coddled him
and he performed all over Europe.

And it seems like only yesterday, in the Kensington Market
at the dog groomer's shop, on Augusta Avenue,
where my beloved dog Lucy used to hang out,
there was a fluffy-coated black and white Vietnamese pig,
as big, as smart, as gentle as a Border Collie:
and nobody knows where he is now.

IV
CHIBOK VILLAGE
False, Forbidden, Allowed
#BringBackOurGirls

Boko (Hausa), False
Haram (Arabic), Forbidden

Let's talk about girls—

First, what is forbidden:
for girls to go to school
for girls to study false knowledge
for girls to bare their heads, show their hair
for girls to play music, hear music
for girls to sit next to boys—
Forbidden.

Second, what is allowed:
for a nine-year-old girl to be taken from her family
for a nine-year-old girl to be raped
for a twelve-year-old girl to be made pregnant, to bear a child
for any girl to be abducted from school
to tie a girl to a tree to die
to strap a bomb to a girl, send her into a village—
Allowed.

I

Eastertime, April 2014, 276 schoolgirls at desks
in a boarding school, writing their final physics exam

to graduate from high school.
Their mothers uneasy, abductions in other villages,
have been reassured, security tight,
their children will be alright, will flourish,
do them proud.
This is the village of Chibok, northeast Nigeria.

Nigeria, populous, rich African nation,
seventh most populous country in the world,
twentieth largest economy in the world,
multi-cultural, multi-ethnic, multilingual,
500 languages, Hausa, Yoruba, Igbo,
English, the *lingua franca* for all.

The dialing code for Chibok village,
partly Christian, partly Islamic, is +234.
You could call one of the mothers whose child has disappeared.
She would ask you to help.
Taken at midnight.
Classrooms set alight.
Taken in trucks to the Sambisa Forest.
Headmistress, Asabe Kwambura, begs
'Boko Haram, have mercy on my students.'

Look, you can see the encampments easily on Google Earth.
Here's Beyoncé, she has started a Twitter account to save our daughters.
But you, listener, reader, can't you help us too?

II

Easter again; three years since my daughter,
our daughters, were taken into the Sambisa Forest.

Some had bombs tied to them, exploded in other villages;
Some died of HIV, some tied to trees, starved to death.
They tell us the Christian girls were murdered.
Our village Chibok has many Christians.
We live peacefully, as villagers, together—
now only a third still alive.

One day, twenty-four ran out of the forest,
a few with babies in their arms.
Their bride price only 6 pounds.
Six British pounds for my daughter.

Esther Yakubu begins to weep about the Boko Haram video
'sent to our village chief; he called us all to watch:
fifty of our girls on the video.
There I saw my daughter—
my first born, my Dorcas:
I thank the Almighty for sparing the lives of some,
my dearest Dorcas among them.'

III

Easter again,
activists are rallying in Abuja, the capital.
Thousands march silently through the streets
red tape across their lips.

Rebecca Samuel begins to cry:
'It's a nightmare for me, every night,
it seems like yesterday, I have heard nothing,
Where is my daughter? Where is Sarah?
Please, please, bring her back.'

2015, Anglican cleric Stephen Davis tries to negotiate
for the release of the seriously ill girls.
Told not to interfere, he leaves the country.

In Borno state, ninety-one more women and girls abducted.
Likely more than 600 held.
2000 claims Amnesty.

IV

14 October, four girls walk from Cameroon to freedom.
They tell us they were raped every day.

5 May, Boko Haram leader Abubakar Shekau shakes his fist,
threatens to sell girls as slaves.

11 May, 130 girls, now in hijab and chador,
faces veiled, displayed as converted to Islam,
offered as exchange for 100 Boko Haram prisoners.
The deal falls apart.

30 May, two raped and kidnapped girls found tied to a tree.
Four murdered girls lie half-buried nearby.
In the north east, in Damasak, in November 2014
Boko Haram abduct more than 500 children.

Over their twenty years, Boko Haram have killed
more than 30,000 people, crippled thousands,
driven 2.6 million from their homes, destroyed health centres,
fire-bombed places of worship,
disrupted markets, agriculture.
Millions face starvation.

In the first three months of 2017,
children carry out twenty-seven attacks,
deadly suicide bombings on villages.

We must repeat, we need to repeat
the facts over and over
#BringBackOurGirls.

Most Chibok girls were taken to the Sambisa Forest,
some were taken to nearby Chad and Cameroon—
'There are no girls from Chibok here on the soil of Cameroon,'
insist Chad government officials, and yet…

October 14, four of the Chibok girls
walk from Cameroon to freedom.
They too were raped every day.

V

A society of contradictions:
imprisonment of gays, rape, torture,
corruption commonplace,
sharia law strong.

Boko Haram—*boko* forbidden, *haram* fake,
or is it the other way around?
Anti-secular, anti-child, anti-girl,
anti-woman, anti-

No one really knows what Boko Haram is,
all know it means—
Displacement, Death, Destruction.

Thousands of children abducted,
only twenty-four schoolgirls released after negotiations.
#BringBackOurGirls, an international movement
has failed to bring back the girls.

A few escape, many pregnant,
some missing, presumed dead,
but not by their mothers weeping, days, months, years:
'Does she live, where is she, can you hear me calling?
My daughter, my daughter, your mother aches for you:
Can you hear me?'

VI

Can we repeat this story until it is no more?
A continuous present: chronology meaningless.
#BringBackOurGirls, the wailing chorus of Chibok mothers.

Let's return to that Easter night, 14–15 April, 2014—
If only it were for the last time.
The Nigerian military knew four hours in advance.
No mobilization.
Not long after Easter, Boko Haram attacked Chibok again
killing fifty people, eleven parents of the stolen girls.

There's more, forgive me if you have heard this before.

The RAF found all the Chibok girls,
offering to rescue them.
The Nigerian Government refused:
It is a Nigerian issue.

VII

May 2016, a young woman, a baby, a man,
severely malnourished, found in the Sambisa Forest:
'My name is Amina Ali Nkeki;
I was taken from school in a truck, sold for a bride price,
4 British pounds, 6 us dollars, 8 Canadian dollars,
I had not known a man. He raped me, and raped me.
We have nothing to eat, my baby might die—
Please take me back to my parents.'

VIII

October 2016, twenty-one Chibok girls released,
negotiations for eighty-three underway.
Easter 2017, nothing.
Not one of the rescued girls reunited with her family—
They are contaminated, they are *boko*,
they are *haram*, pariah.

November 5, 2016, Maryam Ali Maiyanga released with her baby.
2017, Rakija Abubakur found with her six-month old baby
in the Sambisa Forest.
One hundred and ninety-five Chibok girls still captive.
Tens of thousands kidnapped.

IX

Amina lives with her brother on the streets in Maiduguri.
She sells broth and detergent.

All around is the bustle of traffic,
kebab stands, small tea cafes.

In this city, everyone is a victim,
and a collaborator.

Children escaped from Boko Haram have seen
their sisters, brothers, fathers, mothers beheaded.

Amina's older brother was shot.
Taken by Boko Haram, Amina's job was to capture young girls,
crouched in terror in their homes.

In her dreams, she sees one of them:
'She fainted more than once in the truck as they took her away.
For three weeks they left her alone, then one day they came,
took her to one special room in the camp.

While eating, we could hear her cries.
One man after another.
It lasted three days—she died.'

Farms burned by the Nigerian military,
an effort to stop Boko Haram,
also causing famine, dislocation.

Shunned by their community, as bush wives,
escapees are often beaten, driven away.
Girls who have been raped are loathed.

X

Vigilantes in Nigeria track down Boko Haram.
One is a woman named Hannatu.
She joined after her husband was murdered.

'At first I was afraid, now I am not afraid,
I carry my weapons alongside the men.'

Hunting Boko Haram, vigilante groups murder many innocent people:
Impossible to know who is, who is not.

Zara was taken at seventeen.
'The man was strong, raping me every night.
Then with two other girls, rotating rapes.
He told me suicide bombers have a better life in heaven.
It doesn't hurt, it's just like an ant bite.'

XI

Years pass. Eighty girls have been traded.
Not one has been allowed to return to her family:

Paraded for press photographers, they bolster the reputation
of the ailing president, Muhammadu Buhari.

What of international outrage over the school girls' abduction?
Beyoncé? Michelle Obama?

In Abuja, May 2017, BBC interviews Yakubu Nkeke,
head of the Chibok Parents' Association.

He rejoices with the Chibok villagers
at the release of girls, and his own daughter.

Seven children from his family, including his brothers,
have been taken by Boko Haram.

'The people of Chibok spent the whole night
singing and praising God for the girls' release.'

'Will your daughter return to the village?'
Yakubu Nkeke is evasive.
'She will continue her education in September.'

'Have you discussed her time away?'
'Oh no, we do not talk about that.
She hugs me. That is all.
The girls will be distributed in September.'

'How do you feel about Boko Haram?'
'I forgive them; they are human too.
I am a Christian.'

Rebecca Samuel continues to dream of her daughter Sarah.
But Sarah will not return.
She is now *boko*, she is now *haram*.
She is now part of the *harem*
of Boko Haram.

V
I'M YOUR MAN

Well, there were the three of us,
Jules, Larissa and I, at *Snakes and Lattes*
which has a lot to do with the milk of human kindness
in the dark places, where the old serpents lead us,
on the edge of Remembrance Day, talking of Leonard Cohen,

while only a car ride away, along the old road east,
Leonard was preparing himself to be buried
in the old Jewish cemetery, already dead,
as we talked of 'The Famous Blue Rain Coat'

and Alex would come down from the north
to sing for us one last time, to sing for us all,
'The Famous Blue Raincoat', with Rory on guitar,
one last time, for the last holiday party,
the coming holiday party.

So we three were playing a board game called *Concept*,
trying to fathom the American Election,
and Leonard had died, even as we spoke,
and Larissa had spent the night crying
about the animals and the world,
now that the world was trumped.
Jules hugged her close.
We set to on the board game, mesmerized,
putting the question, the auxiliary, the clues
Yes/No/Yes? No/No/No:

So Yes, now it's Remembrance Day, November 11,
I fetch the paper from my front porch,
a red poppy between my teeth,
thinking of all the vets
who have killed themselves
after Afghanistan deployment,

and I unfold the paper, and there he is, Leonard,
sitting on his old iron bed,
in his little old house, in Montréal, near Portugal Square,
surrounded by feathery pillows, and a puffy duvet,
wearing a suit, and a small beret
and The Famous Blue Raincoat
is floating up to the ceiling.

VI

THE HOUSE THAT JACK BUILT:
Post-Traumatic Stress Disorder,
A Brief History

Two beautiful women with long red hair walk toward us
on a country road, near Calgary, Alberta.
Each holds a hand of a small boy in a Superman T-shirt.

Eyelids almost closed, tongue protruding, leaning a little to the right,
the boy pulls into another space, against their hands,
his mother on his right, his grandmother on his left.

The women animated, engaged, the grandmother smiling at the boy,
the younger woman looking toward the older.
Fashionably dressed, tall, slender, long-legged in blue jeans.

The grandmother in a grey long-sleeved cowl-necked sweater
and padded sleeveless grey zippered vest.
Her daughter in a black long-sleeved sweater, with peek-a-boo shoulders.

Across her chest is a purse, on a gold metal chain.
Beyond the trio, fields of grain, like the chain on the young mother's purse,
shimmer in the afternoon light.

She fell in and out of violent relationships, addicted to oxycodone and to heroin.
Four years old, the little boy is from her second marriage.
His twelve-year-old half sister is also under scrutiny.

The smiling woman on the right of the photograph
is a retired member of the Canadian military.
Her father, a stoic military man, refused to discuss his postings to Germany and to Cyprus.

He loved me, but I never felt it.
Our cold relationship I also forged with my own children,
and I was a single mother at the time.

In 1998, my mission was to analyze dental remains of Swissair Flight III,
smashed into the Atlantic Ocean, a few kilometres from Peggy's Cove, Nova Scotia, Canada,
killing all 229 victims.

After each grisly day at the morgue, I'd go home,
take a hot bath, and weep. I was on my own, my daughter was only ten.
I just checked out as a mother.

I love my children, but I didn't know how to feel.
I was cold; I had no emotion, and if I did it was anger.
After diagnosis for post-traumatic stress disorder, I was released from the military in 2010.

I suspect my children and my grandchildren suffer from vicarious trauma,
their deep psychological wounds mimic my own PTSD.

The military acknowledges this growing problem of vicarious trauma,
as new generations struggle with their parents' multiple deployments to Afghanistan,
longest war in Canadian history.

Children becoming depressed, suicidal,
disrespectful of authority,
angry inside, unable to say why.

She looks at her grandson, at her daughter, at herself,
at their harrowing capacity for rages,
at the blood's capacity to convey

through the generations,
through the innocent, through the inexperienced,
experience itself,

and the frustrating cry, the battle, the struggle to heal.

VII

JEAN ST-GERMAIN, *patenteux*
1937–2016

Welcome!
I am Jean St-Germain, *patenteux*—creator, artist, tinkerer—
patenteux suits me just fine. I am an inventor,
entering new spaces.
    Speaking of which, thank you for visiting me here in my Aérodium.
Mind that propeller there. Off you go now.
Weightless at last. Happy silo soaring—
Enjoy the ride!

I was born into a family of eleven children,
couldn't conceive of fewer.
My inventiveness might seem endless
—always a piece of paper, a napkin,
a sketchbook and pencil—
but we had twelve children, each unique—
Diane, Lucie, Gina, Josée, Jean Michel, Sara,
Daniel, Pierre, Nathalie, Anik, Alexandre, François.

They are the invention of my beloved wife, Adrienne Roy.
Sadly, our dear François preceded us,
yet he lives in us all.
What a life we have had together.
One year we lived in an airplane hangar,
right next to a 1930s DC-3 transport.
Moored like an iron angel beside our home.
I was always mad about airplanes, flying, aviation.

I was a paratrooper in the Canadian army.
At home, near Montréal, I taught parachuting,
invented this silo, where you are now floating,
its wind machine helping you defy gravity, as you skydive,
so everyone can experience the thrill of flying.
I built a light plane, a helicopter, even a tractor
to tow cross-country skiers
right up into the air.

Air was not my only interest.
I defied gravity in many ways.
What a fox I was with Revenue Canada.
They opened my safety deposit box, and found only 50 pennies!
But that American tycoon gave me nearly two million dollars
franchising my Aérodome invention:
I was featured in *People Magazine*.
    Even as a teenager, I was famous—

childhoods were full of burping babies, until I came along,
with a condom in a baby bottle,
preventing babies from sucking in air—
no more stomach cramps. The condom collapsed
as the little ones drank. I sold that one when I was a mere boy—
one thousand dollars, a lot of money at that time.
I worked in a laundry—I was a grade school dropout—
twice through grade four was enough for me.

At 17, I joined the Army, posted to Germany.
I was good at all sorts of things, delighted in music,
playing piano, accordion, guitar.
    My children all take something from me—
Daniel invented a mechanized dancing stage for nightclubs,

another's a musician, another in aviation.
All my endeavours, never specializing:
I may not have been all things to all people,

but I took all knowledge for my province,
and I had a really good time.
I wanted my children to enjoy their lives—
have fun growing up together.
    I believed in the power of numbers and in meditation,
built a giant pyramid, meditated standing up for hours.
Then I tried to beat the tables at Atlantic City, worked for a while.
No limits on imagining.

Remember *L'Extra - Terrasse*, my restaurant
just outside Montréal, robots serving customers fast food,
building shaped like a flying saucer?
(Running restaurants however was not for me.)
My pyramid had healing powers,
although folks paid for entry.
Yes, the power of numbers,
but it was not all magic.

Safety throttles for snowmobiles, miniature helicopters,
air flow deflectors for trucks,
mobile construction scaffold systems.
After the restaurant, came a giant roadside cross,
2000 lights, a pilgrimage site, with a wax statue of Jesus
and soil from the Holy Land.
That cost me a pretty penny:
filed for bankruptcy not long afterwards.

My children were happy,
there was always something new.
Tradesmen came and went, with our latest plans,
property littered with miniature machines.
Always considering the elements, and the stars.
Ready always for another ride.
And here you are!
Welcome back!

VIII

ST. JOHN ON PATMOS

Pieter Bruegel, landsman, painter,
my grandfather, a legend,
a kind of god, never came to Patmos,
never watched the sea of humanity
bobbing in the lovely, tempestuous Aegean
but I, Jan, was there.

His world was the land and its richness,
the celebrations of passages,
the seasons, human life,
his angels fell rebellious.

And I think of them,
thrown out of heaven:
Icarus, but it could have been Daedalus,
falling from the sky, those tiny legs
poke from the sea,

as the rest continue their daily rounds.
Skeletons of a defeated army
fill the foreign ground.

Sometimes he enjoyed a late summer day—
his peasants rest askew beneath a tree,
while others harvest a field of gold.

He knew darkness, beauty,
human transience and frailty.

But there's a man in a cave writing—
looking out over the water—
water turbulent, populated—

boats everywhere rising, sinking,
waves rushing higher, higher,
as more people take to the waves
and the sky changes—dark light—
there are sprays of lightning
the sound of thunder,

but he continues to write in the cave—
you can't see him, but he's there:
What does he write with?
What does he write on?
What does he write?

Out there are islands,
too many names to list,
people looking for shelter
making for shore,
many would die
as he continues to write—

Rains come down,
flooding picturesque Symi,
pouring on delicious Panormitis,
threatening Kos, shaking Rhodos
and the Turkish coast—

but the man in the cave is focused on the future,
perhaps for eternity,

not the drownings in the great ocean,
not the dead, in the wave-washed caves of Symi,
not the drowned child, Alan Kurdi, on the beach near Bodrum,
not the fleeing, searching for a new place,
for shelter.

He is writing in the book of life—
he is writing in a book of life—
four men on horseback will appear—
miraculously—
and then a woman, clothed in the sun—

He can't see her step out of the sun,
emerge from waves,
her dress wrapped about her waist.

A man, a stranger, comes down the beach toward her,
offering a bunch of grapes—
but that's another narrative, altogether.

Instead, the man in the cave writes, as he lives it
waiting for that lift out of the turmoil,
out of the ocean of boats,
of humans, reaching, like the man in the cave
for another shore.

IX

MARY FOGG
1920–2016
Visual artist
Eversfield Care Home, Surrey, UK

...thou shalt make the tabernacle
with ten curtains of fine twined linen,
and blue, and purple, and scarlet with...
loops of blue upon the edges...And...taches
of gold...And...brass...And...skins dyed red...
And thou shalt make an hanging for the door...
wrought with needlework.
— Exodus 26:1–36 KJV

We travelled the world, Alan and I,
and we made a grand garden together.
We went to the continent, camping in our old van.
Mornings, I wiggled my toes, as we awoke.

We had many friends, family.
Summer theatre in all weather. So many picnics.
I adored picnics. I've had a nice life.

I was thrifty. I lived through war and depression.
The land of my birth was India, but my childhood was a tent
and an uncultivated dusty farm in Australia.

I knew the uses of things,
I drank the water from boiled vegetables.
And I had a long life.

I used to mix the salad dressing in those small film canisters.
I was never wasteful,
but I did like a good piece of fine Swiss cotton
for my undergarments.

I loved to bicycle,
and the smell of tomato plants in the greenhouse.
Karen and I often took the bicycles out down the dirt road,

and then there were the walks through the muddy fields to Chaldon Church,
the terracotta frescoes; Saxon, they said, but who really knew.

One year Karen's friends, Winston and Andrew, came down from London,
walked to Chaldon Church. Sam was a teenager then,
and he guided them through the fields.

Who can say which child resembles us—we were a family:
there a nose, here a gesture,
there an uncanny expression.

Some would say it was my first born, perhaps because she is female.
Sarah has my kindness and my curiosity, but is less quick to dismiss foolishness.
She knows where I keep my discarded beads, under the staircase at Albury Edge.

Or Sam. He has the Warren Hastings wen, as does his son, my grandson Theo.
Ours is art always. He takes much from me, his high spirits, his energy.
He needs to slow down.

One day when I was looking for him, he had climbed the cherry tree at Albury Edge.

I quilt, I embroider. Real art takes time.
Sam sat with me for eleven days, as I lay dying.
That's 264 hours.

And Charlie, born last, a bit of a late bloomer.
He has his father's steadfastness, attention to detail.
Finally, we were a family, here an intonation, there a passion.

I was Mary Marsh, Mary Eleanor Marsh, Commander in the British Army.
I had many adopted children.
There was Maude, long gone back to America.
We visited her once, Alan and I, all grown up now, even old.

And there's Karen.
All those times we spent in the gardens and the green house,
but she never liked the smell of tomato plants.
Now I'm gone I predict they will be her passion.

And Chris, five years together every week, surrogate son, beloved.
Good times together. Bless him for all the rewriting of my history of quilting.
And he went with me to Arundel in the Care Home van.

What a bore to get everyone strapped in.
It took so long.
But I loved it, my girlhood revisited.

And Robin. We thought he'd become Governor of the Bank of Canada.
Instead, he became a well-known Marxist historian.
Some say the world's most important economist.
Well, that's exactly what Putin would say, isn't it?

Karen married from our house.
Dr Simpson's wife was here from Woodstock that Christmas.
She tried to stop it. Perhaps we should have.

Karen was always a little lost, needed another family Alan said.
Called her his adopted daughter.
Once I saw him pat her on the head, as he entered the kitchen door
after coming off the train from work in London.

She was just sitting there, on a stool shelling peas.
Something in that must have touched him.
Wrote her when he thought she needed fatherly advice.
He took her on more perhaps than she had noticed.

I have loved them all.

Karen came to us each year: no summer without her, some winters too.
She brings me glamorous outfits, that blue silk coat dress, a tie-dyed shawl.
I never know what she will turn up with, or in, or with whom.

These past few years since Alan's death have been hard.
I know Sam blames himself for the shingles which attacked my eyes.
Stress they said, and they shouldn't have.

You see, Alan said to Karen, there has never been divorce in our family.
But human beings are barometers of the times.

Karen came in the fall of 2014, and I said to her why haven't you gotten taller, fatter?
I had all these clothes I wanted her to have, but they wouldn't fit.
We knew that. But I wanted her to know I wanted her to have them.

Senior Commander
Mary Marsh 1944

2014 was a good visit. Karen and I laughed a lot.
I set the table for lunch while she cooked; Chris was joining us.
I found the cheese in the refrigerator and carried it to the table.

What are you doing, Mary? I am putting the cheese on the table.
But Mary, that is not the cheese, that is my hard-boiled egg from breakfast.
We always laughed.

One day we walked down to the housing development.
I flew off the curbs. And I got lost between the aisles of the grocery store.
Karen shopped for coconut milk, so she could make me the chicken curry I loved.
On the way back, I fell in someone's garden trying to show her a flower.
She managed to get me upright. Who knows how.

We walked down Nutfield Road.
There were horses in the far field.
I could see they were brown.
My eyes undimmed for a moment.

The summer of 2015 was glorious; Sam and I at Aldeburgh.
We recapitulated so much of our life together.
I escaped him more than once to walk the shale beach.

Karen didn't come that fall, and I knew Sam knew where she was and why.
But she did come in 2016, and I promised her on the telephone
I would try to stay alive for her visit.

I was in the home by then, no friends, no one to talk to,
all infirm, although they said they were much younger than I.
Thank goodness for Chris's more than weekly visits,
and my sons came too, and Sarah each year, of course.

Before I passed over, life that month was different.
Karen arrived and came to me each week,
between visits to Malta and Glasgow.
She brought us picnics, we sat in the garden the first visit.

I eat very very slowly. Things tumble off my fork.
Do you think I should try to move it faster?
I can't really.

We walked around the garden.
The frame is awkward, but we strolled anyway along the paths.
Then we waited for a cab to take her to the train to London.

She said she would come back after Malta.
For some reason I thought she said Edinburgh.

Time does not exist here.
Was it a week ago a year ago a day ago?
I have no idea.

Someone has come in. I hear someone, but I cannot hear.
I do not have my hearing aids on. Who is it? Who is it?
Mary, Mary, it's Karen.

Oh, what day is it? Have you been to Edinburgh?
No, I am going to Glasgow tomorrow.
I just came back from Malta with Nick.
Oh, I was just sitting here. Yes, you were staring at the apple juice.
Are you okay? Yes, yes.

Mary's night dress is undone; she is not present.
There is a knock at the door, and Maria enters.
Mary, Mary, where is your bra?

Who are you, a relative? I'm a visitor.
I can see that.

Mary, let's get you dressed, it is nearly noon.
What do you want to wear?
I need the necklace that matches my dress.

Karen goes to the wooden case.
She tries to pry open the secret door with scissors.
Don't break my scissors I say to her.
She thinks I can't see!

One necklace—then another, then another.
That one Sam brought me from Ethiopia.
That one you brought from Tuscany, thirty years ago.
That was my mother's, I can't feel guilty about the elephant.
It's old, Mary, as long as it's before 1965, it's okay.

Maria is finally done dressing me and fussing.
She thinks she owns me.
She's bossy, but a sweetie.
From some island somewhere in the Atlantic or the Pacific.

Today is the "free" bar; let's go down and drink. It gets busy quickly.
Hello Mary, hello Mary. Here's the program for the week.
A woman enters and leaves behind a leaflet.

Will you read it to me? It's so boring here, but I try to go to these events.
Chris comes with me. I wish they would let him move his Crosswords here on Mondays.

Will you sit with me after I order a cab? I must be back in London by 4 PM.
Alright. Mary, where are you going?
We are going to the reception. That is the elevator. This way.
You'll need to turn around.
Alright.

Karen orders the cab. There is a sofa there.
So many sit on this sofa all day, waiting for someone who never comes.
They fall asleep.

A woman comes into the reception area.
She is looking for the loo. Karen shows her where it is.
A moment later she comes out and asks again for the loo.
One of the staff appears and helps her to the same door again.

We wait for the cab.
I tell Karen I have often sat on this sofa all day,
waiting for someone who never comes.

What will you do this afternoon?
I suppose I will just sit here and doze.

See you next week.

X

ROB STEWART
1979–2017
Warrior

There is grandeur in… endless forms most beautiful and most wonderful…
— Charles Darwin, *On The Origin of Species*, Chapter XIV (1859)

First, a goldfish, then a monitor lizard,
next a boa constrictor, named Mali,
his little boy's bedroom a menagerie
of the beauteous living forms of the world.
Fell in love with his first shark at the age of eight.
At 14, he was a scuba diver,

and his whole family followed suite.
A bit of a nerd, surrounded by fish tanks,
memorizing entire books on animals.
He travelled to Kenya, Jamaica, Madagascar,
Costa Rica, in Africa collected a black mamba,
one of the world's most venomous snakes.

A big kid at heart, always optimistic,
his surfer dude drawl disguising a stutter:
'Check it out, guys, we'll make environmental activism cool,'
and he did.
As a photographer he travelled the globe,
taught himself how to film.

He loved the reefs and the sharks, and the rain forests
and was chased by gun-toting, shark-fin-mafiosi,
caught dengue fever, West Nile virus, flesh-eating disease,
tuberculosis, but was always upbeat.
He believed we could change. He had faith.
Anything was possible.

Building community for global change.
Passion, imagination, empathy and courage:
These were who he was, said Sea Warrior/
Sea Shepherd Paul Watson.
In 2002, Rob Stewart armed himself with a camera,
the most powerful weapon in the world.

In 2017, off the coast of Florida,
on a rebreather, he made three deep dives,
the rebreather says it all—
not some alien invader blowing bubbles,
one with the water and the sharks,
one with the world he fought for.

Photographer, award-winning film-maker
writer, conservationist.
Changing the world:
one frame at a time.

XI
PIKANGIKUM,
Then and Now

The children of Pikangikum are dancing,
dancing the seven grandfather teachings,
truth, courage, humility,
honesty, respect, wisdom, love,
telling their stories through movement.

Pikangikum, Pick-AN-gee-kum,
small Ontario town, Ontari-ari-ario—
Canada's heartland.

Pikangikum, Ojibwe community,
highest original language retention
of all Ontario First Nations,
fly-in community, northwest of Red Lake,
northwest of Thunder Bay, small Ontario town,
once called suicide capital of the world.

In the beginning, hunting, fishing,
five or six families live from the land,
everything hand-made, clothes, tools, dwellings:
land, spirits, people, one.
60,000 years, spirit rocks, hand-crafted,
60,000 years, self-sufficient, intimate life.

On the Berens River, four communities,
Pikangikum, Poplar Hill, Little Grand Rapids, Pegaussi.
Each four clans: caribou, sturgeon, pelican, skunk.

Each family, a log house, hand-hewn.
Each community a sacred drum, held by the elders,
heartbeat of your mother, heartbeat of the community,
heartbeat of the land.

Honesty, respect, stories, elders,
wise women central to its life:
Elders sing, tell stories, keep the sacred drum,
beating, pounding, belonging.

Hudson's Bay Company sets up a post:
Trading—everyone benefits.
Trapping buys goods, establishes credit.
Commodity culture begins.
Hudson's Bay factors and families
live in the community, log cabins, fishing,
chuckling by the sacred rocks.

Schools, health officials, police, together, sharing the life.
One day a teacher, a principal, buys the sacred drum,
leaves the village.
Disconnect.

Christians, Mennonites, Catholics, United Church-folk
threaten spirits with hell-fire, damnation.
Gradually people turn away.
Community grows faster, faster.
More and more children are born,
welfare cheques based on numbers.
Elders no longer tell stories: distance, disconnect.

Children leave families, go to residential schools,
return, cannot tell of rapes, beatings,
threats for speaking their own language—
shame, drink, breakage.

How to tell your mother, your father, your grandfather—
How to tell the people you love most,
how to tell of beatings, of buggery—
Shame.

3,000 souls on a collision course.
2,000 under twenty-five—
Helplessness, hopelessness,
drugs, suicide pacts:
Young girls, not twelve, hang themselves,
buried in their own front yards.

Imagine these children, schoolmates with knives,
patrolling their own communities
to cut down a brother, a sister, a friend, a peer.
Imagine the life of this child?

Four in five homes, no running water,
no sewage disposal; more than 2,000 jobless,
national disgrace.
Clean water will not be enough.

Once it was bottomless:
Fish, fowl, fur, giant trees, metals, fuels.
Impossible to fathom boundaries.
Land of the Giant Beaver.

On the Berens River was a sacred gathering place,
the giant grandfather rock:
Mennonites destroyed the site, cursed it as pagan.
Hudson's Bay factors left the community—
Hudson's Bay taught 'nature worship sinful',
yet native hunting and trapping was the backbone of its wealth.

How to keep the land whole,
physical, mental, spiritual;
how to teach hope, lives have value.

Lust persists, preachers, police,
exiled languages, fire, brimstone, rape:
the story continues while the children
drunkenly ride All-Terrain Vehicles
and their houses have no toilets, no water,
and the animals have all gone,
and the elders no longer tell stories,
no longer keep a sacred drum.

It's all on Facebook, and YouTube:
fights with the Ontario Provincial Police officers,
themselves with post-traumatic stress disorder,
smashed glass, hurled rocks, destroyed cars,
blaring fire alarms.

Is reconciliation bumping bloody fist to fist
while a wealthy country tolerates no toilets,
no water, no jobs for its people.

Ask ourselves, what it means 'our first world',
with no game for hunters,

no food, no shelter for birds, fish, animals,
no clean water, no elders with stories:
children take their rite of passage,
journey to adulthood, sniffing gas.

There is an epilogue:
the children of Pikangikum are dancing,
dancing their own stories;
dancing out intergenerational trauma,
dancing for truth, courage, humility
wisdom, respect, honesty, and love.

XII
ON A GOLDEN ASIAN PEAR
For John Evans,
1943–2019
Actor

In nineteen days you will be dead,
but here at a little table on a sunny sidewalk
on College street at Palmerston
I survey the menu.
It's the Bar Raval, and the offerings are all tapas:
little offerings, some delicious, just like life.

I'm sitting with Rita, and we are pleased with ourselves
on this glorious fall afternoon. It's Yom Kippur, Wednesday,
the ninth of September, noon, but we don't talk about atonement,
we discuss the future, our writings, our hopes,
my feelings of being underutilized,
her wisdoms offered in response.

A woman approaches with a white plastic bag.
She's an ordinary looking woman, no need to be on the alert
as she begins to speak, 'Hello, I'm the Queen of England,
could you spare some change?'
Rita opens her purse and hands Queen Elizabeth
a twenty dollar bill.

Queen Elizabeth opens her eyes wide, opens her bag,
in it displays a glorious golden Asian pear.
In nineteen days, further west on College street, Sidecar,

another restaurant, will close, never to reopen;
all tender dreams of humanity: Rita's gift of a twenty dollar bill,
the beggar woman with the Asian pear, stolen from FreshCo,
your desire, unfulfilled, to play Prospero.

Some rough magic haunts us,
the deep moans round with many voices:
I enter the funeral home guestbook—
My picture, my seasons in the key of J,
all times, all pageants insubstantial
love played in an unknown key:

Ave atque Vale, Hail and Farewell,
May your dreams be rich and strange—
though no tempest, even in its roaring,
will wake you, sleeper,
while day continues to chase the night.

XIII

LITTLE BY LITTLE
For Michael Mitchell
Writer/Photographer/Friend
Raconteur Extraordinaire
1943–2020

Poco a poco.
Little by little, hour by hour,
day by day,
you wait for your departure,
canny in choosing firecracker day,
The Queen's Birthday, Victoria Day,
a celebratory day, calendar day, admirably Canadian
as you sail off before dawn, take yourself to the other place
just as the sun is preparing his own passage.

Ride on the billowing waves;
sail on through winds and the tide.
You were a sailor in many guises—
wily like Odysseus, a lover
of women, and the siren's song.

Sail on through gates of ivory and gates of horn—
some dreams, they say, pass there and do deceive
and some, they say, do come to pass.
Little by little, the light fades, the prism loses its colour—
we will think of you in your boats, frail and tough
saluting the morning's minion—
teaching us all how to die.

Your books—lost landscapes, lost times, lost animals,
lost people, great elegies to the mess,
while we hurry on the path to self-destruction—
turning each of us always to fundamentals.
    You watch Ossie in his Jamaican garden
surrounded by frangipani, guava, and coffee trees,
his voice a whisper, 'I'm sorry I'm taking so long to die.'

My last visit to your hospital room:
still so many laughs, your room licensed:
who would have thought a hospital would sanction a private bar.
You were irresistible.
And after all these months, looking so much more handsome
without your hair: I'm going home soon, you said,
as soon as I can get strong. They'll let me out.
Look, here's a rubber band, I am building muscle,
doing isometrics in my bed.

Weeks pass, and long telephone conversations.
Where are you, you would ask? Which room? What is it like?
Oh and yes, soon, very soon, I am feeling better.
What are you reading? What are your writing?

But the light is changing,
Day by day, hour by hour, minute by minute.
Poco a poco.

XIV

AMOR OMNIA VINCIT
For Jane Somerville-Caspari,
Community Builder, Publisher, Friend
1949–2020

Michy asked me why I had written no elegy for you,
my old dear friend, decades together—
from your most golden years, your brilliant years
to the last troubling times——

I evaded the question, although sometimes I said
there was never space, clarity—
so much pain, destruction, her beauty
shattered, horrifying,
tumours, vicious, relentless.
Her bravery and her decline writ together
like twisted iron rods.

Perhaps I was waiting for the evidence
in your library, and your always immaculate home—
Casa Loma of Lawrence Park, your beloved called it,
and it was one of your passions, your many passions.

Of course, there were your children, and your grand-children,
and your lover, your husband of fifty years, and community,
friends, your running, your cooking, your making of books—
you were one of the prolific,
and you were beautiful, irrepressible, and antinomian:
in good and bad ways, of course.

I spent hours sorting your library,
a gift for your husband, advising on dispersing
clothes and masses of miscellaneous.
Who would have imagined beneath the order, so much chaos.
Who would have imagined meeting the tumour growing,
decade after decade, silently, covertly,
decimating that brilliant and beautiful creative mind.

And so beloved Jane, I sing to you fare-thee-well, on your final journey:
remember us together on horseback at a gallop,
runaways, while an earthquake shook Cuba.

Remember us together, one New Year's, scuba-diving, in Curaçao
then later carefully placing stones on nameless graves
helping the souls of the dead stay free of demons,
in an ancient windy Jewish cemetery.

Remember us together sailing in Costa Rica,
watching a mother whale, and her two babies,
gloriously breach.

Or simply remember us sitting in a little bistro
on College street, in Toronto, talking of books
and business, and everything wonderful,
starting with the letter A.

XV
FISHERMAN'S REUNION
PRODIGAL

All over is white snow,
But you can smell the spring

Somatsumaru, 'Twin Pines',
its name on launching, symbol of aged marital harmony.
Its secret name was *Prodigal*,
searcher after secrets, mysterious wayfarer.

Though he was only twenty, perhaps Kou Sasaki knew
they would not be together forever;
still he waved the ceremonial flag
over his new scallop boat, welcoming it to the fleet,

setting sail with the others, on the great adventure,
from the harbour of the Japanese fishing port of Ofunato.
Year after year, they were one, as he searched the sea,
married, honed his skills.

Then came the earthquake, and the great tsunami,
11 March 2011, a year of disasters, natural and man-made,
world-wide, the scream of buildings torn apart,
millions of tons of debris filling the Pacific Ocean,

19,000 dead borne along on the tides,
including the wife, and young son, of Kou Sasaki,
and the small fishing boat, *Prodigal*,
Twin Pines, on a highway of water.

Two years pass, and 7000 kilometres,
Twin Pines arrives in Klemtu, British Columbia,
to a new life in harmony with the Spirit Bears
of the west coast islands,

magnificent white bears, paradoxical black bears,
unique in the world. Peaceful at anchor in the harbor,
Twin Pines, renamed *Japanese Drifter*, joins the community
of the Spirit Bear Lodge.

No longer a fishing boat, now a fisher of souls,
taking tourists searching for the Spirit Bear,
black bear with white fur, Kermode bear,
ghost bear, giver of miracles, Healer.

In the big house, Kitasoo dancers greet Kou Sasaki
and his new wife Shuko, with ceremonial songs.
Seeing *Prodigal* for the first time in four years,
Kou Sasaki shouts, *There, oh there!*

He jumps into the empty boat weeping.
Thanking the Kitasoo people of Klemtu
for saving his boat, welcoming him,
he gives them *Twin Pines'* ceremonial flag.

The Kitasoo take Kou and Shuko in search of the Spirit Bear.
On each side of the boat, swimming, guiding them
toward an inlet rich in herring eggs
is a marine wolf.

They round a corner of the inlet,
toward the mouth of a fresh water creek,

a large white bear, with her two newborn black cubs
is fishing for spawning salmon near the edge of the sea.

Kou Sasaki and Shuko,
with their sponsor from Vancouver, Yoshi Karasawa,
stand in the community's gathering place,
thanking their hosts for their dances and songs,

they sing a soft song of renewal:
All over it is white,
But you can smell the spring.

NOTES ON POEMS

The fifteen elegies in this collection are based in part on my travels, both near and far, including to the indigenous archipelago of Haida Gwai, in the northwest Pacific Ocean, off the west coast of Canada, and to the eastern Mediterranean, its Turkish coastline and some of its islands, Rhodos, Symi, and Panormitis (looking toward Patmos). I have spent time as well in the Middle East, in Israel, the West Bank, Jordan and Turkey. My own academic research took me often for long periods to the UK, where two generations of the Fogg family took me in, tutored me, and cared for me.

News accounts both online and in print include the *New York Times*, *The Guardian*, *The Globe and Mail*, and *The Toronto Star*. They were especially important for my long poems about Pikangikum (XI), Grassy Narrows (II), and the kidnapped Nigerian school girls of Chibok Village (IV). Because the statistics regarding destruction by the jihadists Boko Haram in northeast Nigeria change and increase constantly, it was decided to leave the numbers at their 2018 level, where articles in the *New York Times* were especially important to me. Information is easily found online as to the current levels of destruction of crops, and human beings. Children are still being captured, families and villages destroyed, even as I write. Long after I finished my Chibok poem, I read Edna O'Brien's deeply affecting novel *Girl* (2019).

The position of chief in the First Nations community of Grassy Narrows (II) is not hereditary but elected. Several chiefs have had the surname Fobister. Steve Fobister (d. 2018) was elected chief five times. His funeral is in my poem. Other Fobister chiefs of Grassy Narrows include Simon (d. 2019), and Randy (2021) who has recently signed an agreement with the federal government for health care facilities in their community.

'The Pigs in Question' (III), blends two news stories about the animal activist Anita Krajnc, who was arrested twice by police, once for attempting to give pigs water on a hot day (June 2015), and then trying to help the pigs escape after the truck taking them to slaughter overturned (October 2016). Anita Krajnc's cases were dismissed. The presiding judge issued a moving decree: 'Compassion is not a crime.'

ACKNOWLEDGEMENTS

I am grateful for support in the writing of these texts from Black Moss Press in 2019 through the Ontario Arts Council's Writer Recommender Grants.

I am also grateful to the hard-working team at Eyewear Publishing/The Black Spring Press Group for accepting my book, seeing it through publication, and for the deeply intuitive capabilities and continuous care of my editor Cate Myddleton-Evans.

Versions of five of these elegies appeared in print in 2018 and 2019: 'Pikangikum' in *untethered magazine*, Spring 2018, 'Mosul, Child and Bicycle' and 'I'm Your Man' in the anthology, *release any words stuck inside of you*, (Applebeard Editions, 2018). Another version of 'I'm Your Man' was also published online by The League of Canadian Poets, Poetry Pause, 18 July 2019. Versions of 'Mosul, Child and Bicycle', 'St John on Patmos', and 'The House That Jack Built, PTSD, A Brief History' appeared in *The Friendly Voice*, vol.4, issue 8 (December 2019).

'Pikangikum' was nominated for a Pushcart Poetry Prize (USA) in 2018. A gathering of thirteen of these elegies was short-listed for the 2019 International Beverly Prize for Literature (Eyewear Publishing/ The Black Spring Press Group, London, UK).

Ongoing thanks to the City of Toronto for two short-term residencies (2018 and 2019) at Artscape/Gibraltar Point, on the Toronto Islands, by the Gibraltar Point Lighthouse. Many of my books have been conjured and have grown in the quiet and the fellowship of this artists' retreat, on a series of sand-spits, in the harbour of Canada's biggest city.

The use of the photograph of Mary Fogg (IX) has been kindly permitted by her son, Sam Fogg.

ABOUT THE AUTHOR

Karen Mulhallen's publications have been translated into Spanish, French, Bosnian, Italian and Turkish. She has published 24 books, including 18 collections of poetry, as well as numerous essays on fashion, travel and art criticism. In addition to editing anthologies, she has worked as a magazine columnist, book editor, and magazine editor, including *The Literary Review* (London), Somerville House Books (Toronto), as well as *The Canadian Forum*, and *Descant*. Please visit www.karenmulhallen.com.

Lightning Source UK Ltd.
Milton Keynes UK
UKHW031005020622
403884UK00003B/7